Discovery KIDS™

DANGEROUS ANIMALS

Sandy Creek
NEW YORK

Sandy Creek
387 Park Avenue South
New York, NY 10016

SANDY CREEK and the distinctive Sandy Creek logo are trademarks of Barnes and Noble, Inc.

© 2009 by Parragon Books Ltd
© 2009 Discovery Communications, LLC. Discovery Kids, DiscoveryFacts and related logos and indicia are trademarks of Discovery Communications, LLC, used under license.
All rights reserved. discoverykids.com

This 2012 custom edition is published exclusively for Sandy Creek by Parragon Books Ltd.

All rights reserved. No part of this publication may be reproduced, stored in a retrieval system or transmitted, in any form or by any means, electronic, mechanical, photocopying, recording or otherwise, without the prior permission of the copyright holder.

Written by Cathy Jones and Janine Amos
Reading consultants: Christopher Collier and Alan Howe, Bath Spa University, UK

ISBN 978-1-4351-4155-1
Printed in Guangdong, China
10 9 8 7 6 5 4 3 2 1 Lot
03/08/2012

Contents

Sharks
Sharks 6-25
Quiz 26
Quiz answers 102
Glossary 28

Jungle Animals
Jungle Animals 30-49
Quiz 50
Quiz answers 104
Glossary 52

Dinosaurs
Dinosaurs 54-73
Quiz 74
Quiz answers 106
Glossary 76

Wild Cats
Wild Cats 78-97
Quiz 98
Quiz answers 108
Glossary 100

Index 113

Parents' notes

This book is part of a series of non-fiction books designed to appeal to children learning to read.

Each book has been developed with the help of educational experts.

At the end of each section is a quiz to help your child remember the information and the meanings of some of the words and sentences. There is also a glossary of difficult words relating to the subject matter in the book, and an index.

SHARKS

What is a shark?

Sharks are fish that live in seas and oceans across the world. Some sharks are tiny, others are giants. Some are gentle and some are fierce.

Sharks don't have bones. Their skeletons are made from light, stretchy cartilage.

fins

jaws

gills

Sharks breathe through slits called gills.

There are hundreds of kinds of sharks. Here are just three of them.

Wobbegongs hide on the ocean floor. They are well camouflaged.

Dogfish have long, slim bodies to slip through the water.

tail

Angel sharks have flat bodies. They also hide on the ocean floor.

DiscoveryFact™

Sharks have been living on Earth for 400 million years. They were around at the time of the dinosaurs.

Amazing sharks

Can you imagine a fish that has a head shaped like a hammer? Or one that can gobble up a sea lion whole? Sharks are some of the world's most amazing creatures.

The bullet-shaped mako shark is the fastest fish in the ocean. It can swim at 45 miles per hour.

The strange hammerhead shark has eyes on each side of its head. It swings its head from side to side to get an all-around view.

DiscoveryFact™

The great white shark eats other sharks for dinner—along with whole penguins, seals, and sea lions.

The gentle whale shark is the world's biggest fish. It weighs as much as two elephants.

Teeth and tails

Teeth and tails are two of a shark's most important weapons. They are designed to help it catch prey.

Sharks always have a mouth full of teeth. When one set of teeth wears out, there is another set waiting.

A nurse shark has long, curved teeth for hooking prey.

A shark's tail helps push it along. Fast swimmers have curved tails. The thresher shark has a long, strong tail to knock out its prey.

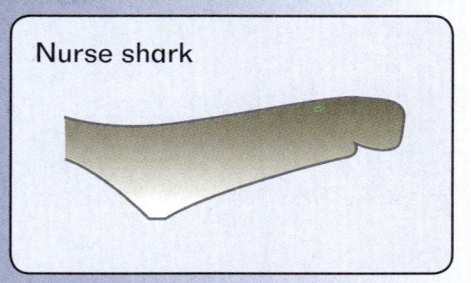

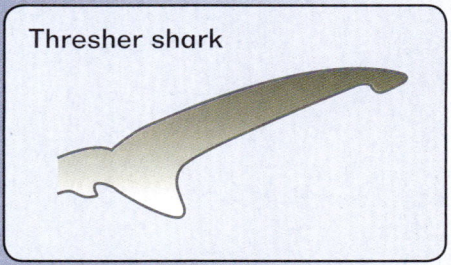

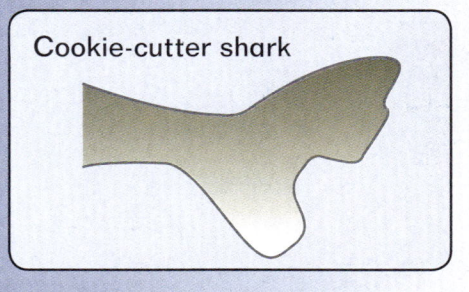

Tiger shark	Nurse shark
Porbeagle	Thresher shark
Great white shark	Cookie-cutter shark

DiscoveryFact™

The small cookie-cutter shark swims up to a larger fish, takes a bite out of its side (the shape of a cookie), and swims away again very quickly!

Swimming

Most sharks are graceful and powerful swimmers. Their smooth bodies are perfect for moving underwater. Sharks swim in S-shaped movements, powered by their tails.

Fins on each side of a shark's body help it steer.

The stiff fin on a shark's back helps with balance.

The shark's long tail beats from side to side, pushing the shark forward through the water.

Inside most fish is an air-filled swimbladder. It keeps the fish afloat. Sharks don't have swimbladders. Most have to keep swimming or they sink.

DiscoveryFact™

The prehistoric shark Megalodon may have been up to 65 feet long. Here is one of its huge teeth next to the tooth of a modern shark.

Blue shark

The blue shark is a long-distance traveler. It swims hundreds of miles every year, searching for food or to mate.

The blue shark has a bright-blue back and a white tummy. These colors help to hide it in the ocean.

Blue sharks hunt with their mouths wide open, trapping fish in the corners. They are slow swimmers but can move very quickly when they attack.

DiscoveryFact™

One blue shark made a trip of almost 4,500 miles from New York to Brazil. That's a lot of swimming!

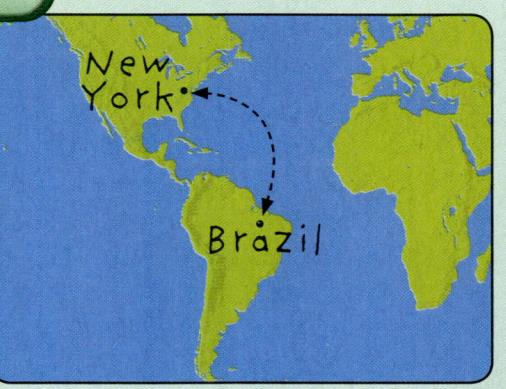

The blue shark feeds on small fish, such as sardines, and on squid (shown left). It lives in warm and cool oceans all over the world.

Hunting

Sharks are always seeking out their next meal. They can see, hear, touch, and smell, just like people. But their senses are much more powerful.

Touch
A lateral line along their sides helps sharks pick up movements in the water around them.

Hearing
A shark's ears can hear sounds traveling through the water.

All of these words appear in the book. Try to match the word and picture stickers.

gills   wobbegong   dogfish   angel shark   fin

great white   hammerhead   whale shark   mako

nurse shark   cookie-cutter shark   *Megalodon* tooth

blue shark   squid   tail   dinosaur   pup   teeth

killer whale   seal pup   mermaid's purse   stingray

submarine   penguins   surfboard   sea lion   friends

DiscoveryFact™

An extra sense lets sharks pick up the electric signals given off by fish. This sense is particularly powerful in hammerhead sharks.

Sight
A shark's eyes can see well in dim underwater light.

Smell
Sharks have good noses. They can sniff out blood half a mile away.

Great white

Great white sharks are giant hunters. They feed on animals such as sea lions and seals, as well as on smaller sharks.

Newborn great whites are already 5 feet long. Young sharks eat other fish, such as mackerel and tuna.

Great whites swim near the surface to hunt. But they can dive deeper than a submarine.

Great whites have 3,000 teeth. Each one is about as long as your finger.

DiscoveryFact™

A killer whale like this, and people, are a great white's only enemies.

19

Family life

All baby sharks are born from eggs. The eggs of most sharks grow inside their mother. A few kinds of shark lay their eggs on the ocean floor, safe inside tough egg cases.

Shark babies are called pups.

DiscoveryFact™

A blue shark mother can give birth to 50 or more babies at a time.

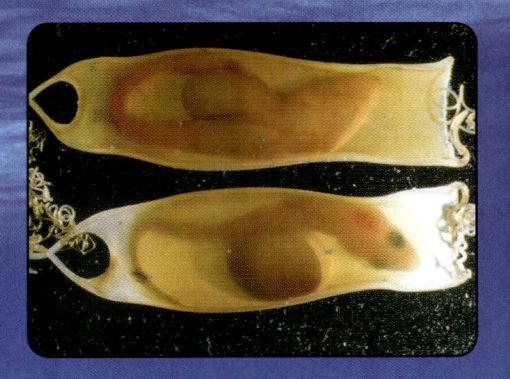

Dogfish eggs are protected by an egg case called a mermaid's purse. The babies grow inside, feeding on the egg yolk.

Lemon shark eggs grow inside their mother. She gives birth to tiny pups, which soon swim off to find food.

Hammerhead

The hammerhead's flat, T-shaped head makes it look different from any other shark. Hammerheads swim together in groups called schools.

Most hammerheads live in warm oceans, off the coast of Australia and Central America.

The hammerhead's favorite food is the stingray. It holds the ray down with its "hammer" and takes a bite.

DiscoveryFact™

Baby hammerheads are born with their heads bent backward, so they don't get stuck inside their mother.

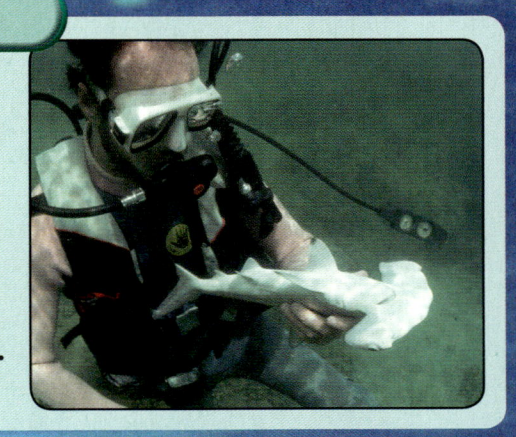

Hammerheads swing their heads from side to side as they swim, picking up smells and sounds in the water.

Their eyes are far apart on their huge heads.

23

Are sharks dangerous?

Most sharks don't eat people. But some sharks, such as the great white, the bull shark, and the tiger shark do attack. There are fewer than 100 attacks every year worldwide.

To stay safe, swim with your friends. Never swim if you are bleeding, because blood attracts sharks.

People are putting sharks in danger. We kill them for food and for sport.

If you see a fin above the water looking like this it means that a shark is near you.

DiscoveryFact™

A swimmer on a surfboard can look like a seal — to a shark.

25

Sharks Quiz

Now try this quiz!
Find the answers on page 102.

How long have sharks been living on Earth?

(a) 40 years
(b) 400 years
(c) 400 million years

Which shark is the fastest fish in the ocean?

(a) The mako shark
(b) The great white
(c) The wobbegong

Which parts of a shark's body help it steer?

(a) The fins
(b) The teeth
(c) The gills

What do young great white sharks eat?

(a) Plants
(b) Fish
(c) Penguins

What is a hammerhead shark's favorite food?

(a) Chocolate
(b) Seaweed
(c) Stingrays

What are baby sharks called?

(a) Pups
(b) Fry
(c) Spawn

Glossary

Cartilage Strong, stretchy material that forms a shark's skeleton.

Fins The wing-like parts of a fish that help it steer and balance.

Gills The parts inside a shark's throat that let it breathe in water.

Lateral line A line of tiny hairs along a shark's body. The lateral line picks up movements in the water.

Pups Newborn sharks.

Senses To see, hear, taste, touch, and smell. Sharks have an extra sense for picking up electrical signals from their prey.

Swimbladder A tiny air-filled bag that helps some fish to float. Sharks don't have swimbladders.

Yolk The yellow part of an egg that feeds the growing baby shark.

Discovery KIDS

JUNGLE ANIMALS

Life in the jungle

The jungle is a hot, steamy forest. It is also called the **rain forest**. Tall trees grow up to 230 feet above the forest floor. The rain can take 20 minutes to reach the ground.

The forest floor is dark because the tree branches block out the sun.

DiscoveryFact™

There are almost 10 million species of animal living in the rain forest, but only about 1.5 million have been named.

- Birds nest and bats roost in the tallest trees.

- Apes, monkeys, and sloths climb in the canopy.

- Snakes, frogs, and **insects** live in the branches and trunks.

- Wild cats, anteaters, elephants, and other large animals prowl the forest floor.

- Crocodiles, turtles, and fish swim in the swamps and rivers.

Rain forests grow between the tropics and the equator, the hottest part of the earth.

Jungle animals

All kinds of animals live in the jungle, such as **mammals**, **reptiles**, birds, and fish. Insects are the largest group of animals in the jungle.

Some animals have **adapted** so well to life in the jungle that they cannot live anywhere else.

Mammals, such as the golden lion tamarin, are covered with fur and feed their babies milk.

The Indian gharial is a reptile. It hunts for fish in the river. It lays eggs on dry land.

DiscoveryFact™

Piranha fish are small, about 10 inches long. But they have rows of sharp teeth. A school of piranhas can eat an animal as large as a sheep in minutes.

The harpy eagle is probably the largest flying rain forest bird. Its feathery wings measure up to 6½ feet when they are spread out. It can carry away a monkey or sloth in its long talons.

Hunter and hunted

Life in the jungle can be hard. Animals that eat plants and insects are hunted by small meat-eating animals. These small animals are hunted by bigger **predators**.

The jaguar's spotted coat acts as **camouflage**. It eats other animals, such as the giant anteater.

The giant anteater has a long snout and sticky tongue—good for scooping up ants and termites.

Leaf-cutter ants can carry leaves 50 times heavier than themselves. They bury pieces of leaf and eat the fungus that grows on them.

DiscoveryFact™

The poison dart frog is a brightly colored **amphibian**. Its bright colors warn enemies that it is poisonous to eat.

The Amazon

The largest rain forest in the world is in South America around the Amazon River. It is filled with a lot of colorful life.

Capybaras belong to the same rodent family as mice and rats. They grow up to 2 feet tall.

DiscoveryFact™

Vampire bats feed on the blood of other animals.

The colorful, noisy toucan has a strong beak. It can easily open nutshells to eat the kernel inside.

The anaconda is the heaviest snake in the world. It can grow to 37 feet long. It squeezes its prey to death, then eats it whole.

The rhinoceros beetle is the strongest animal in the world because it can carry 850 times its own weight. It grows to over 2 inches long.

Monkeys

Monkeys are **primates**, like us. They have hands like ours with thumbs that bend away from their fingers. Their eyes are at the front of their head. They live in family groups called troops.

These chimpanzees are grooming each other to keep clean and to relax.

The largest monkey in the world is the mandrill. It grows up to about 3 feet tall. The male mandrill has a colorful face and bottom, which get brighter when it is excited.

DiscoveryFact™

The owl monkey is the only monkey that is active at night and sleeps in the day. Its big eyes help it see in the dark.

The smallest monkey in the world is the pygmy marmoset. It is only 6 inches long, not counting its 7-inch long tail.

The Congo

The Congo is the second largest rain forest in the world. Running through the rain forest is the second largest river in the world, the Congo River.

Gorillas are our closest relatives in the animal world. They spend most of their time on the ground, walking on their knuckles for support.

Like its relative the giraffe, the okapi has a very long tongue for pulling food from high trees and thorny bushes.

A chameleon changes the color of its skin to blend into the surroundings if it feels threatened.

All of these words appear in the book. Try to match the word and picture stickers.

golden lion tamarin   Indian gharial   poison dart frog

harpy eagle   vampire bat   bandicoot   owl monkey

anaconda   rhinoceros beetle   piranha fish

giant anteater   leaf-cutter ants   clouded leopard

margay   okapi   chameleon   giant millepede

tree kangaroo   Bengal tiger   peacock   cassowary

orangutan   water dragon   giant tree frog

ocelot   gorilla   jaguar   toucan   mandrill

DiscoveryFact™

The African giant black millipede can grow to 15 inches and has two pairs of legs on each segment of its body.

Wild cats

Rain forest cats are hunters. They hunt alone at night. They have good night vision and mark the forest trails with their **scent** to warn off other animals.

Tigers are the largest cats in the world. The Bengal tiger can grow up to 10 feet long. It hunts for wild boar, oxen, and monkeys.

DiscoveryFact™

The margay spends its whole life in the trees hunting birds and monkeys.

The clouded leopard is a good climber. It can run down a tree trunk headfirst.

The ocelot may look like a pet cat, but it is twice as big. It is also very fierce. It hunts small deer, rabbits, and fish.

Indonesia

Indonesia is a ribbon of 17,000 islands in the Indian Ocean. About one-half of the land is covered in jungle. There are over 3,500 species of animal living here.

Orangutans live in the rain forest trees. At night, they make a nest to sleep in. They eat mainly fruit.

The deadly king cobra grows up to 18 feet long. Its two fangs can inject poison into its prey.

The peacock raises its magnificent tail feathers to attract a peahen to mate with.

DiscoveryFact™

The water dragon is 2 feet long. It can run away quickly on its back legs and hide underwater for up to 90 minutes.

Snakes

Rain forest snakes are good at hiding. They slither under fallen leaves, hide in hollow tree trunks, and wind themselves around overhanging branches. They smell prey by flicking their tongue.

The cobra is a poisonous snake. When it is in danger, it makes itself look bigger by raising its head and puffing out its hood.

The deadly coral snake lives in the trees and on the forest floor. One bite from this viper snake is enough to kill an adult. It grows up to 3 feet long.

DiscoveryFact™

Snakes shed their skin as they grow.

The green tree snake finds its food in the trees, swallowing frogs and lizards headfirst.

47

Australia

The Australian rain forest is home to many animals that are not seen in the rest of the world.

DiscoveryFact™

The cassowary is the largest land animal in Australia at 5 feet tall. It is a bird but it cannot fly.

Tree kangaroos are good climbers and can jump from branch to branch. The baby kangaroo, called a joey, is carried in its mother's belly pouch.

The giant tree frog is the biggest tree frog in the world. It grows up to 4 inches long.

Like a kangaroo, the bandicoot carries its babies in a pouch. The bandicoot's pouch is on its back instead of its stomach.

49

Jungle Animals Quiz

Now try this quiz!

Find the answers on page 104.

Which snake squeezes its prey to death?

(a) Anaconda
(b) Coral snake
(c) Green tree snake

Which monkey is the smallest?

(a) Chimpanzee
(b) Pygmy marmoset
(c) Owl monkey

Why does a chameleon change the color of its skin?

(a) For fun
(b) When it feels threatened
(c) To attract a mate

What do vampire bats feed on?

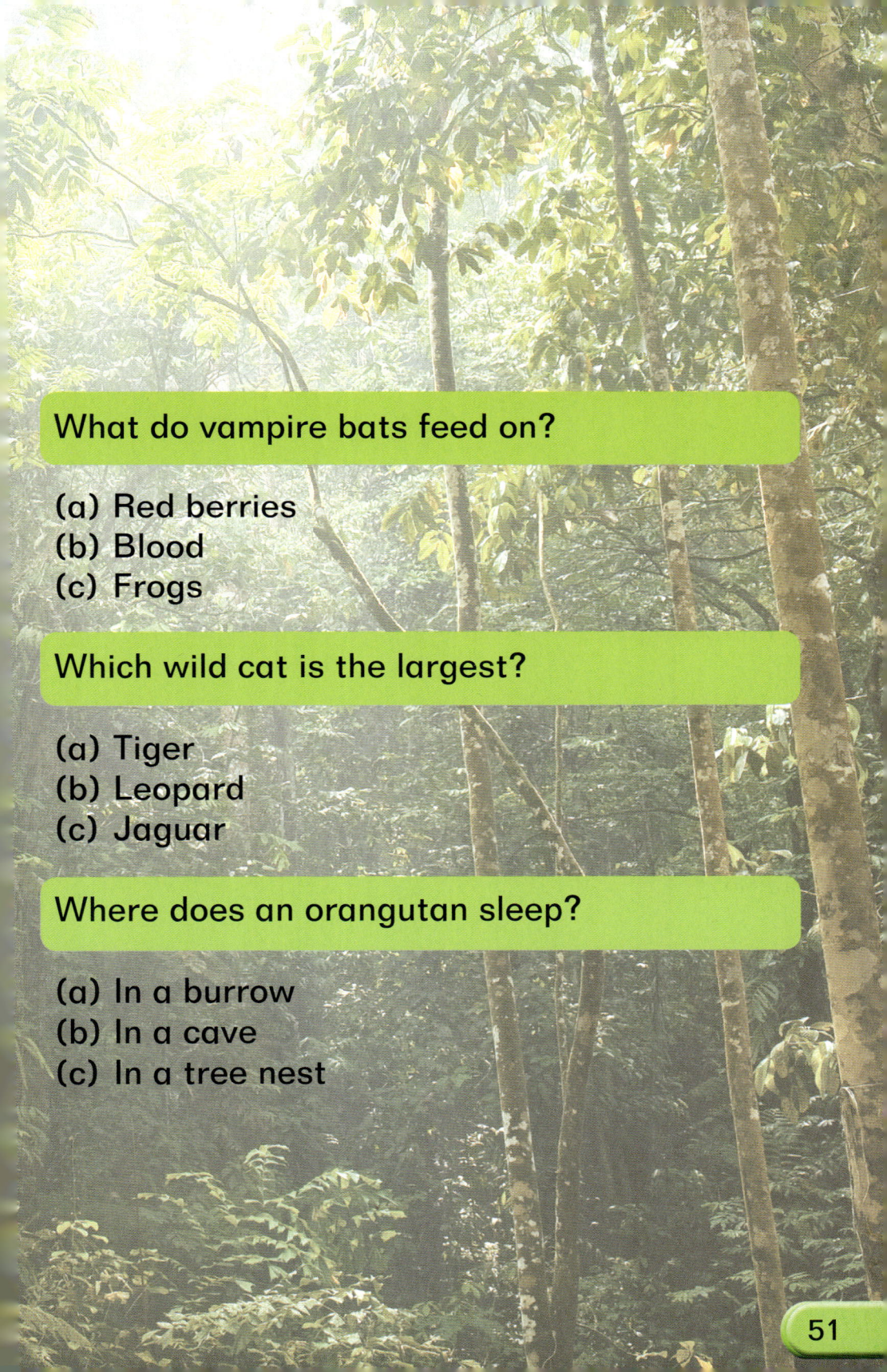

(a) Red berries
(b) Blood
(c) Frogs

Which wild cat is the largest?

(a) Tiger
(b) Leopard
(c) Jaguar

Where does an orangutan sleep?

(a) In a burrow
(b) In a cave
(c) In a tree nest

Glossary

Adapted — Changed in a way that helps the animal to survive where it lives.

Amphibians — A group of animals (such as frogs) that lay eggs in water and can live on land.

Camouflage — An animal's pattern or color that helps it hide against the background.

Insects — A group of small animals with six legs. Many insects have wings.

Mammals — A group of animals that have a backbone, give birth to babies, and feed them milk.

Predator — An animal that hunts another animal for food.

Primates — A group of animals that includes humans, monkeys, and apes.

Rain forest — An area of evergreen forest near the tropics where there is a lot of rainfall.

Reptiles — A group of animals covered with scales that includes lizards, snakes, and crocodiles.

Scent — The smell that an animal leaves to tell other animals it has been in a place.

Discovery KIDS

DINOSAURS

What is a dinosaur?

Dinosaurs were reptiles that walked on Earth millions of years ago. Some dinosaurs were tiny, like birds. Others were giants—the largest land animals the world has ever seen.

Giganotosaurus (above) was the biggest dinosaur ever to have lived. Some of its teeth were longer than your hand.

DiscoveryFact™

Over thousands of years the bones, teeth, footprints, and even poop of dead dinosaurs turned to rock. We call these fossils.

The first fossil of a dinosaur tooth ever discovered belonged to meat-eating *Megalosaurus* (below).

Today, dinosaur skeletons are displayed in museums.

Dinosaur world

Earth's history is split into lengths of time called periods. There were different kinds of weather, plants, and animals in each period.

The **Triassic period** was hot. Palm trees, conifers, and mosses grew on Earth.

Eoraptor lived in the Triassic period.

DiscoveryFact™

The Triassic, Jurassic, and Cretaceous periods belong to one length of time called the Mesozoic era. Dinosaurs ruled the land in the Mesozoic era.

In the wet **Jurassic period**, forests grew. *Diplodocus* and other large plant eaters had plenty to eat.

The **Cretaceous period** was cooler. Flowering plants grew and there were more kinds of dinosaur than ever before.

Diplodocus lived in the Jurassic period.

Velociraptor lived in the Cretaceous period.

Different dinosaurs

Dinosaurs were large or small, heavy or light. Some had smooth bodies, others had spikes and horns. No one knows exactly how many kinds there were.

Velociraptor was a meat eater. It could run fast. Its short front legs were good for grabbing and holding prey.

DiscoveryFact™

Plateosaurus could rear up on its back legs to reach leaves high in the trees!

Ankylosaurus was covered with plates and spines. It was twice as wide as it was tall.

The plant-eating *Ankylosaurus* could defend itself against meat eaters with the bony club at the end of its tail.

Dinosaur diets

Some dinosaurs ate the leaves of plants and trees. Other dinosaurs fed on any animal they could catch.

Allosaurus was a large meat eater. It had pointed teeth and powerful jaws.

Apatosaurus bones have been found with *Allosaurus* teeth marks on them.

Brachiosaurus was a plant eater. This dinosaur had a long neck, like a giraffe. It may have moved about in a herd, or group.

DiscoveryFact™

Ornithopod dinosaurs had beaks, like ducks. The beaks were perfect for chopping off plants and leaves.

Stegosaurus

Stegosaurus was a peaceful dinosaur—with a dangerous tail. Long spikes at the end gave it good protection.

Stegosaurus was hunted by meat eaters such as *Ceratosaurus* (right). If attacked, it hit out with its long, spiked tail.

Stegosaurus

Stegosaurus was a slow-moving plant eater. It lived in herds, feeding on leaves and ferns, such as these.

The bony plates on its back may have kept it cool, or they may have attracted other *Stegosaurus* dinosaurs.

The plates may have turned red when it was excited or afraid.

Family life

Dinosaur babies were born from eggs. Some mothers cared for their young. Others left the babies to look after themselves.

Maiasaura made a nest by scratching a hole in the ground.

All of these words appear in the book. Try to match the word and picture stickers.

Deinonychus   Ceratosaurus   Velociraptor   skull

Diplodocus   Giganotosaurus   Ankylosaurus   duck

Eoraptor   palm tree   Brachiosaurus   Allosaurus

Apatosaurus   Tyrannosaurus rex   ferns   banana

explosion   fossil   skeleton   Stegosaurus   nest

Megalosaurus   Maiasaura   volcano   egg

Iguanodon   Triceratops   Plateosaurus   leaf

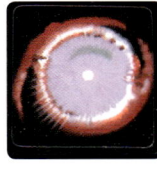

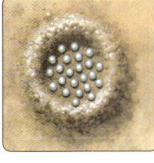

DiscoveryFact™

The biggest dinosaur eggs were from *Hypselosaurus*. They were the size of a basketball.

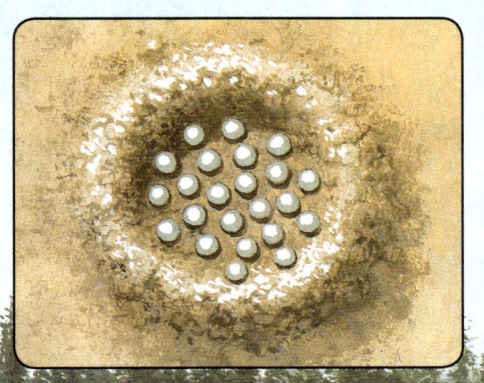

Maiasaura mothers laid about 25 eggs. They stayed near the eggs to protect them.

Maiasaura mothers covered their eggs with leaves to keep them warm.

Triceratops

Triceratops was a horned dinosaur with a frill around its neck. It fed on plants. The frill was used to show off to other dinosaurs.

Triceratops would protect its babies. Its long, sharp horns could spear an enemy's flesh.

Triceratops was hunted by *Tyrannosaurus rex*. Marks made by *Tyrannosaurus* teeth have been found in *Triceratops* bones.

The name "triceratops" means "three-horned face." *Triceratops* had a huge skull. Its neck frill was made of solid bone.

Fierce or friendly?

Some dinosaurs were peaceful plant eaters. Others were fierce hunters.

Like deer do today, *Iguanodon* fed on plants and leaves. These dinosaurs had big, spiked thumbs for holding down branches.

Small but fierce *Deinonychus* may have hunted in packs to bring down large animals.

Iguanodon lived in family groups.

DiscoveryFact™

Iguanodon could bend its smallest finger across its hand to help it grab on to its food.

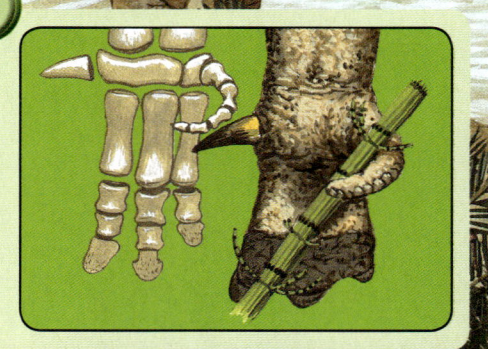

Tyrannosaurus rex

Tyrannosaurus rex was the king of the meat-eating dinosaurs. It had a huge head, with powerful, bone-crunching jaws.

Its mouth was filled with 50–60 pointed teeth. Some were as long as big bananas and they were very sharp.

DiscoveryFact™

This dinosaur's arms were so tiny they didn't reach its mouth. But it could grab hold of its prey from behind.

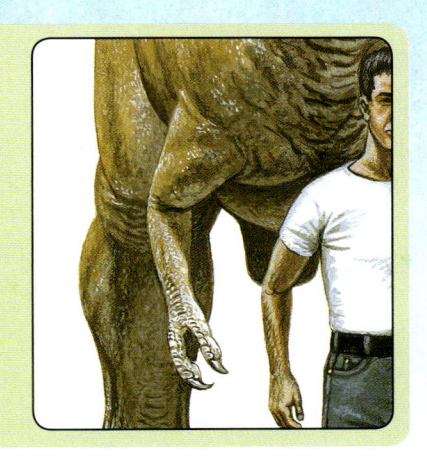

Tyrannosaurus hid in the trees and then surprised its prey.

Dinosaur death

About 65 million years ago all the dinosaurs died out, or became extinct. Experts are not sure why.

Perhaps a huge rock fell from space and dust clouds blocked out the sun. It may have become too cold for dinosaurs to live.

If a huge star exploded in space, deadly rays could have reached Earth and killed the dinosaurs.

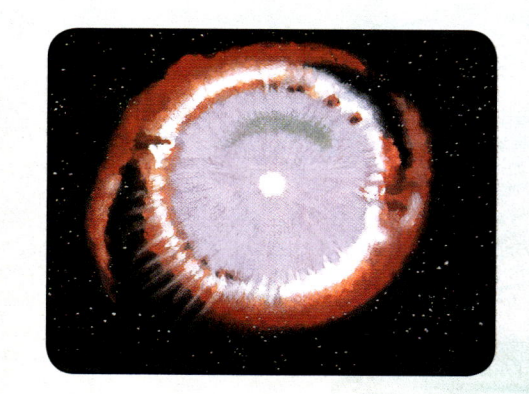

A lot of volcanoes were erupting 65 million years ago. Poisonous smoke could have killed the dinosaurs.

DiscoveryFact™

Thousands of rocks from space have been found on Earth.

73

Dinosaurs Quiz

Now try this quiz!
Find the answers on page 106.

Which was the biggest dinosaur ever to have lived?

(a) *Megalosaurus*
(b) *Tyrannosaurus rex*
(c) *Giganotosaurus*

What did *Allosaurus* eat?

(a) Meat
(b) Plants
(c) Potato chips

How many teeth did *Tyrannosaurus rex* have?

(a) 10–20
(b) 50–60
(c) 150–160

How long ago did the dinosaurs die out?

(a) About 650 million years ago
(b) About 65 million years ago
(c) About 6 million years ago

Which dinosaur laid the biggest eggs?

(a) *Triceratops*
(b) *Maiasaura*
(c) *Hypselosaurus*

Which period of time did *Diplodocus* live in?

(a) The Triassic
(b) The Jurassic
(c) The Cretaceous

Glossary

Cretaceous period From 144 to 65 million years ago.

Extinct When an animal or plant has died out completely so that there are none left anywhere on Earth.

Fossil A part or print of an animal or plant that has been turned to rock. Fossils can be millions of years old.

Jurassic period From 206 to 144 million years ago.

Pack A group of dinosaurs that hunts together.

Plate A flat piece of bone on a dinosaur's body.

Prey The animals that a dinosaur eats.

Reptile An animal with dry, scaly skin. Most reptiles lay eggs with hard shells.

Skull The bone in a dinosaur's head that protects its brain.

Triassic period From 250 to 206 million years ago.

Discovery KIDS

WILD CATS

What is a wild cat?

A wild cat is a mammal with a coat of fur. Wild cats live in most parts of the world. Wild cats eat meat and are smart hunters.

mane

The **lion** is one of the biggest wild cats. Only male lions have manes.

paw

claws

DiscoveryFact™

A tiger is the largest wild cat. Siberian tigers are the biggest cats of all.

The **Scottish wild cat** is about the size of a pet cat.

A **cheetah** is the fastest wild cat—and one of the world's fastest animals.

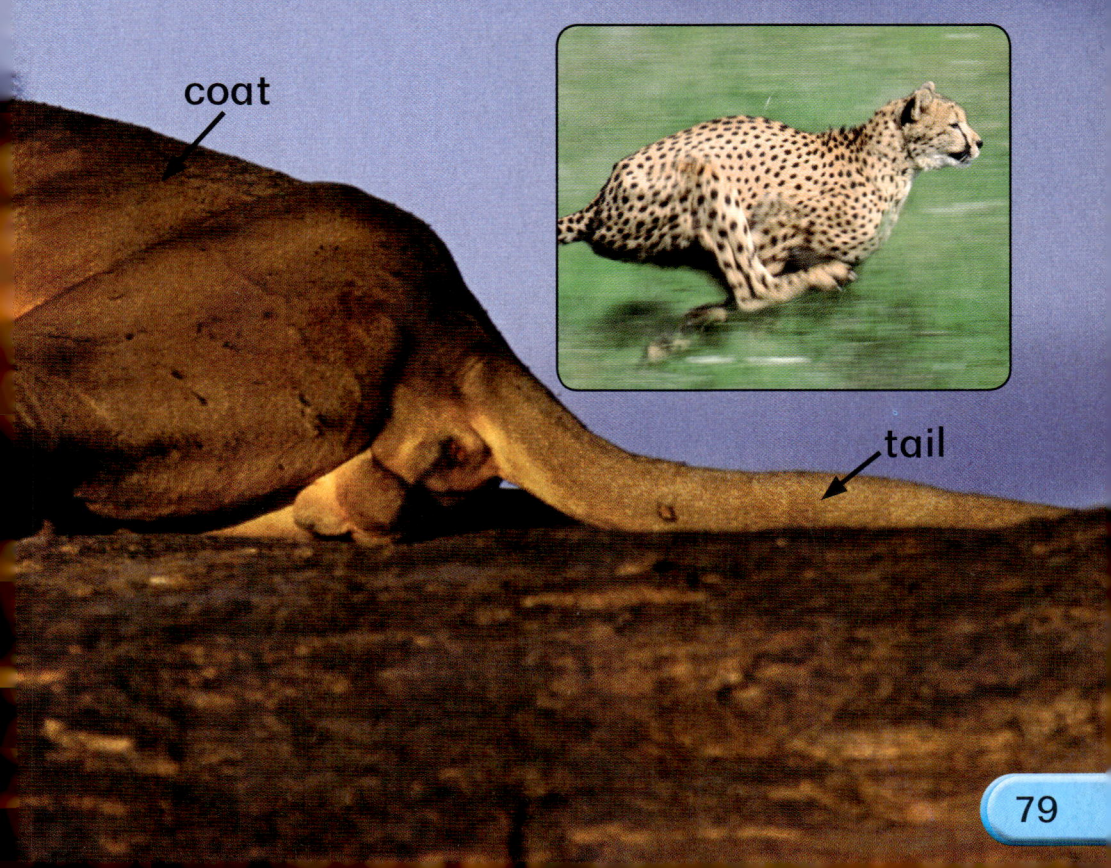

coat

tail

Types of wild cat

There are lots of different kinds, or species, of wild cat. Some are a solid color. Some are spotted or striped.

Tiger
The tiger is a big cat. It is orange with thick, black stripes.

Ocelot
The medium-sized ocelot has both spots and stripes.

DiscoveryFact™

Over short distances, the cheetah can run as fast as a car!

Mountain lion (puma)
The mountain lion, or puma, has a solid gray or brown coat.

Lynx
The lynx is medium-sized. It has a short tail and furry ears.

Leopard
The leopard is a big cat with spots called rosettes.

Wild world

Wild cats live in many parts of the world—in hot deserts, cold mountains, and thick forests. Each species of cat is suited to the place in which it lives.

Forests—jaguar
Jaguars live in forests. They are good tree climbers. Their long tails help them balance.

DiscoveryFact™

Forest jaguars have dark fur for hiding in the shadows.

Mountains— snow leopard

The snow leopard can live in high, cold places. It has thick fur to keep warm.

Deserts—bobcat

The bobcat has furry feet to protect it from the hot ground.

Family life

The babies of most kinds of wild cat are called cubs. The mother protects them and keeps them warm.

Mothers move their cubs out of danger. They carry them gently in their mouths.

DiscoveryFact™

Lion cubs are covered in spots! Their spotted fur helps hide them from enemies.

Mother cats clean their cubs by licking them.

At first the cubs feed on milk from their mother.

Cubs play-fight to practice hunting skills.

Lion

Lions live in family groups called prides. Father lions protect the pride, warning off strangers with loud roars. Lionesses (female lions) do most of the hunting.

Lions live together as one big family. The biggest prides live in grasslands, where they hunt large animals such as zebras.

DiscoveryFact™

Lions spend about 20 hours a day resting—or taking a catnap!

A father and mother lion look different from each other. The father has a shaggy mane around his head.

This picture shows a pride of lions drinking at a water hole.

Hunting

Wild cats are made for hunting. They have good senses. They can see, hear, and smell their prey from far away.

Cats move quickly and silently when they hunt.

Their weapons are their strong jaws and long, curved claws.

All of these words appear in the book. Try to match the word and picture stickers.

male lion   tiger   Scottish wildcat   cheetah

stripes   mountain lion   lynx   ocelot   leopard

forest jaguar   snow leopard   bobcat   jaguar

cub   mother   lioness   pride   serval   tail

spots   buffalo   ear   desert   mountain   forest

paw print   grass   leaf   Iberian lynx

DiscoveryFact™

The serval has such good hearing it can hear small animals moving underground!

Mother cats take their cubs on hunting trips. The cubs learn by watching and copying their mother.

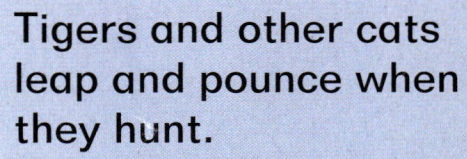

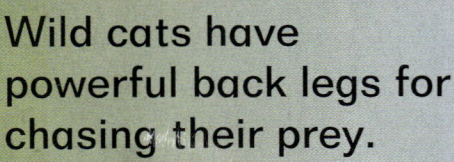

Tigers and other cats leap and pounce when they hunt.

Wild cats have powerful back legs for chasing their prey.

Tiger

Tigers are big and powerful cats—but they are hard to see in their wild homes. Their striped coats blend in with the grass and leaves.

Tigers are good swimmers. On hot days they keep cool in water.

DiscoveryFact™

Fewer than 1,000 Siberian tigers live in the wild today. People have killed many of them.

Tigers can climb trees to keep watch for their prey. When hunting, they watch their prey from the shadows, then rush out and attack.

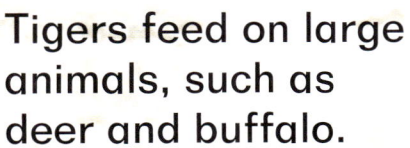

Tigers feed on large animals, such as deer and buffalo.

Keep off!

Cats move across the same area of land every day. This area is called a territory.

Big cats roar to warn others to keep off their territory.

DiscoveryFact™

Experts track wild cats by following paw prints in the earth.

Cats rub their furry bodies against trees. The scent from their fur stays on the tree.

Cats mark out their territory. They leave behind their smell, or scent, by spraying.

Leopard

Leopards are strong cats and good climbers. They spend a lot of time hiding in trees, resting, and watching for prey.

DiscoveryFact™

Sometimes leopards attack from above, then drag their prey into the branches for a treetop meal.

Leopards rest in trees. Their spotted coats help them hide in the leaves.

Leopards hunt alone and at night. They live in forests, on grasslands, and in the mountains.

Leopard cubs shelter in dens in hollow trees, rocks, or caves. Their mother looks after them.

Taking care of wild cats

The world's wild cats are in danger. People have hunted them for their fur or destroyed their habitats (the places where they live).

Some wild cats live in reserves, where they are kept safe from hunters.

DiscoveryFact™

Tourists can visit some reserves. It is an amazing way of seeing wildlife up close.

People have trapped and killed snow leopards for their fur. Today there are laws to protect them.

There are only 100 Iberian lynxes left in the wild. Their habitat is now protected land.

Wild Cats Quiz

Now try this quiz!
Find the answers on page 108.

What do wild cats eat?

(a) Meat
(b) Cookies
(c) Plants

Which is the fastest wild cat?

(a) The lion
(b) The tiger
(c) The cheetah

Where do jaguars live?

(a) Forests
(b) Deserts
(c) Mountains

What is the name of a family of lions?

(a) A pack
(b) A pride
(c) A school

How many Siberian tigers live in the wild today?

(a) Over 1 million
(b) Over 10,000
(c) Under 1,000

Where do leopards like to rest?

(a) In a bed
(b) On the ground
(c) In a tree

Glossary

Coat   The fur of a wild cat.

Cub   A baby wild cat.

Den   A wild cat's home, such as a cave or a hollow tree.

Lioness   A female lion.

Mammal   An animal with hair or fur, which feeds its babies on milk.

Mane   Thick fur around the neck of a lion.

Prey   The animal that a wild cat hunts for food.

Pride   A group of lions that live together.

Reserve   Land where wild cats can live in safety.

Senses   To see, hear, taste, touch, and smell.

Species   Animals of the same kind. All lions belong to one species, all tigers belong to another.

Discovery KIDS

QUIZ ANSWERS

Answers – Sharks

Find out if you got all the questions correct!

How long have sharks been living on Earth?

(c) 400 million years

Which shark is the fastest fish in the ocean?

(a) The mako shark

Which parts of a shark's body help it steer?

(a) The fins

What do young great white sharks eat?

(b) Fish

What is a hammerhead shark's favorite food?

(c) Stingrays

What are baby sharks called?

(a) Pups

Answers – Jungle Animals

Find out if you got all the questions correct!

Which snake squeezes its prey to death?

(a) Anaconda

Which monkey is the smallest?

(b) Pygmy marmoset

Why does a chameleon change the color of its skin?

(b) When it feels threatened

What do vampire bats feed on?

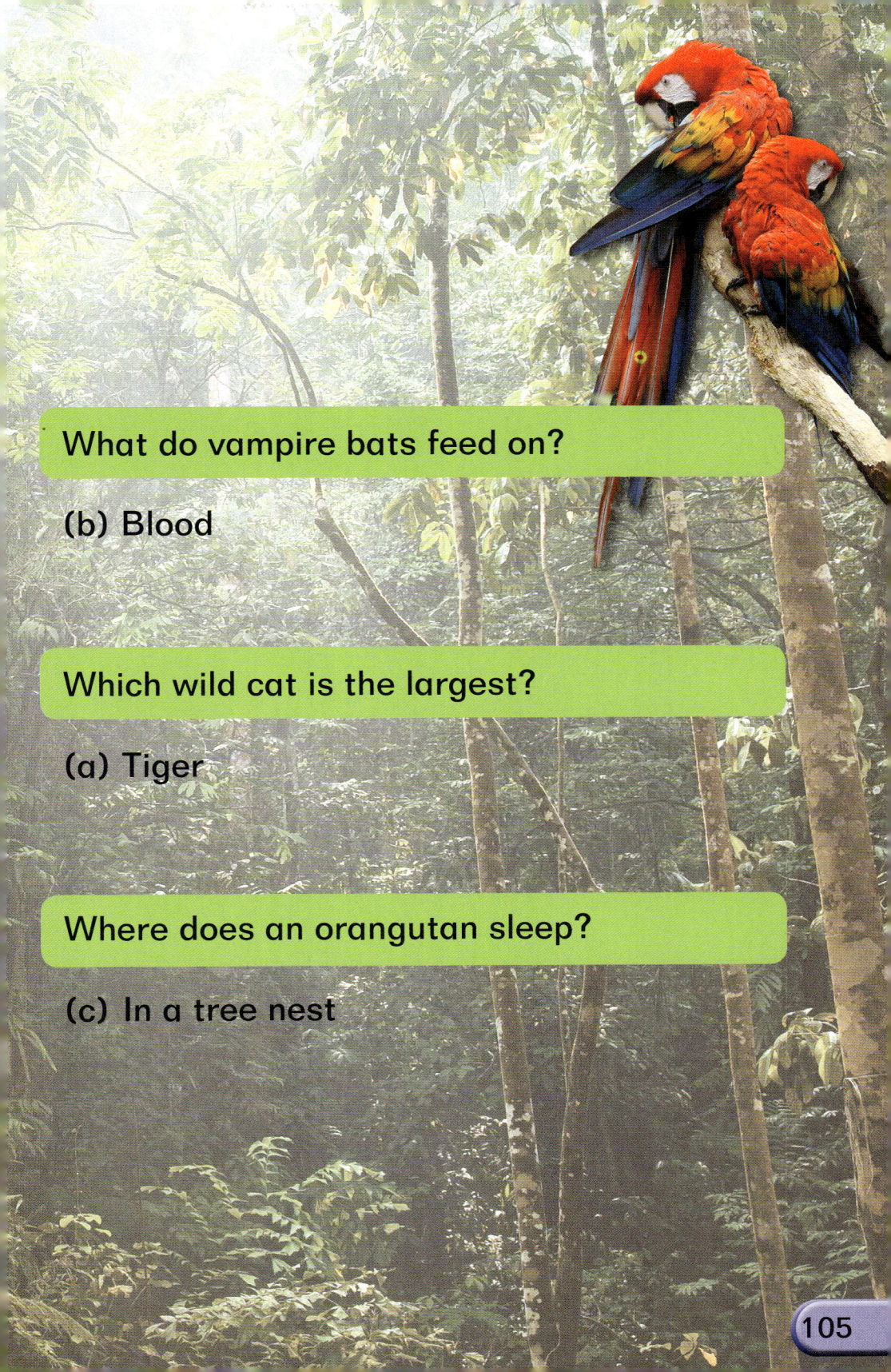

(b) Blood

Which wild cat is the largest?

(a) Tiger

Where does an orangutan sleep?

(c) In a tree nest

Answers – Dinosaurs

Find out if you got all the questions correct!

Which was the biggest dinosaur ever to have lived?

(c) *Giganotosaurus*

What did *Allosaurus* eat?

(a) Meat

How many teeth did *Tyrannosaurus rex* have?

(b) 50–60

How long ago did the dinosaurs die out?

(b) About 65 million years ago

Which dinosaur laid the biggest eggs?

(c) *Hypselosaurus*

Which period of time did *Diplodocus* live in?

(b) The Jurassic

Answers - Wild Cats

Find out if you got all the questions correct!

What do wild cats eat?

(a) Meat

Which is the fastest wild cat?

(c) The cheetah

Where do jaguars live?

(a) Forests

What is the name of a family of lions?

(b) A pride

How many Siberian tigers live in the wild today?

(c) Under 1,000

Where do leopards like to rest?

(c) In a tree

Acknowledgments

t=top, c=center, b=bottom, r=right, l=left

Sharks

p.1br Tim Davis/Corbis, p.5tl Jeffrey L.Rotman/Corbis, p.3t Denis Scott/Corbis , p.5 Amos Nachoum/Corbis, p.6-7 Tim Davis/Corbis, p.6 DLILLC/Corbis, p.7tl Jeffrey L.Rotman/Corbis, p.7tr P.Ginet-Drin/Photocuisine/Corbis, p.7m Norbert Wu/Getty Images, p.8bl Denis Scott/Corbis, p.9tr Tim Davis/Corbis, p.9bl Louie Psihoyos/Corbis, p.10 Denis Scott/Corbis, p.10bl Gary Bell/Zefa/Corbis, p.11br Getty Images/National Geographic Creative, p.12-13 Carson Ganci/Design Pics/Corbis, p.13cl Tim Davis/Corbis, p.13br Jeffrey L.Rotman/Corbis, p.14-15 Background Ralph A. Clevenger/Corbis, p.14-15 Amos Nachoum/Corbis, p.15bl Jeffrey L.Rotman/Corbis, p.16-17 Jeffrey L.Rotman/Corbis, p.16bl Jeffrey L.Rotman/Corbis, p.16br Stephen Frink/Corbis, p.17tr Denis Scott/Corbis, p.17bl P.Ginet-Drin/Photocuisine/Corbis, p.17br Stuart Westmorland/Corbis, p.18-19 DLILLC/Corbis, p.18br Amos Nachoum/Corbis, p.19tr Stephen Frink/Corbis, p19br Tom Brakefield/Corbis, 20 Tobias Bernhard/zefa/Corbis, 21cl Douglas P.Wilson; Frank Lane Picture Agency/Corbis, 21cr Douglas P.Wilson; Frank Lane Picture Agency/Corbis, 22-23 Denis Scott/Corbis, p.22bl Carson Ganci/Design Pics/Corbis, 23tr Jeffrey L.Rotman/Corbis, 24-25 Creasource/Corbis, 25br Rick Doyle/Corbis, 25tl Dimaggio/Kalish/Corbis, 25tr DLILLC/Corbis, 27t Amos Nachoum/Corbis.

Additional images used on sticker sheet: Third row, fifth picture: Gavriel Jecan/Corbis, Fourth row, sixth picture: Bernard Brenton/Dreamstime, Fourth row, seventh picture: Stuart Westmorland/Corbis, Sixth row, second picture: Philip Perry; Frank Lane Picture Agency/Corbis

t=top, c=center, b=bottom, r=right, l=left

Jungle Animals

p.30-31 istockphoto/ SZE FEI WONG, p.30bl istockphoto/ Kenneth O'Quinn, p.31 tr istockphoto/ Finn Brandt, p.32-33 istockphoto/ Ray Roper, p.32 b istockphoto/ Erik van Hannen, p.33 cl Getty Images/Joel Sartore, p.33 cr istockphoto/Simon Podgorsek, p.34-35 Getty Images/Tim Laman, p.34 cl istockphoto/Sondra Paulson, p.34 b Getty Images/Peter Lilja, p.35 br istockphoto/Steve Geer, p.36-37 Getty Images/M G Therin Weise, p.36 br istockphoto/Michael Lynch, p.37 tr istockphoto/Roberto A Sanchez, p.37 cl Getty Images/ Gary Braasch, p.37 br istockphoto/Tokle, p.38-39 Getty Images/VEER John Giustina, p.38 cl istockphoto/Catharina van den Dikkenberg, p.39 tr Getty Images/Art Wolfe, p.39 cr istockphoto/Michael Lynch, p.40-41 istockphoto/Guenter Guni, p.40 cl istockphoto/Gary Martin, p.40 bl istockphoto/Kenneth O'Quinn, p.41 br AFP/Getty Images, p.42-43 Getty Images/Jami Tarris, p.42 br Getty Images/Carol Farneti-Foster, p.43 tr istockphoto/Dieter Spears, p.43 cr Getty Images/ Tom Brakefield, p.44-45 istockphoto/George Clerk, p.44 br Getty Images/Tom Brakefield, p.45 br Getty Images/Frans Lemmens, p.46 Getty Images/Bnsdeo, p.47 cl Getty Images/William Weber, p.47 tr Getty Images/Jim Merli, p.47 b Getty Images/Joel Sartore, p.48-49 istockphoto/Susan Flashman, p.48 bl Getty Images/Jason Edwards, p.49 tr National Geographic/Getty Images

Dinosaurs

Illustrated by:
Norma Burgin, Mark Dobly, Graham Kennedy, Peter Konarnysky, Damain Quayle, Neil Reed, Pete Roberts (Allied Artists), James Field, Terry Riley (SGA), Mike Atkinson, Chris Forsey, Rob Shone, Q2A Media

Photography credits
t=top, c=center, b=bottom, r=right, l=left

p.55tr Garry Gay/Getty, p.55br Paul A. Souders/Corbis, p.63tl Acerable/iStock, p.65tr samkee/iStock

Wild Cats
t=top, c=center, b=bottom, r=right, l=left

p.77 Joe McDonald/Corbis, p.79tl Kevin Schafer/Corbis, p.79tr Steve Austin; Papilio/Corbis, p.79br Renee Lynn/Corbis, p.80-81 Randy Wells/Corbis, p.80br Darrell Gulin/Corbis, p.81tl DLILLC/Corbis, p.81tr Joe McDonald/Corbis, p.81bl Alan & Sandy Carey/zefa/Corbis, p.81br Joe McDonald/Corbis, p.82-83 Frans Lemmens/zefa/Corbis, p.83tl Jim Zuckerman/Corbis, p.83tr Alan & Sandy Carey/zefa/Corbis, p.83br DLILLC/Corbis, p.84-85 Joe McDonald/Corbis, p.85tl Gabriela Staebler/zefa/Corbis, p.85tr Michael Kooren/Reuters/Corbis, p.85c Tom Brakefield/Corbis, p.85br Renee Lynn/Corbis, p.86-87 Paul A. Souders/Corbis, p.86br Stephen Frink/Corbis, p.87tl Randy Wells/Corbis, p.87tr Gallo Images/Corbis, p.88 DLILLC/Corbis, p.89tr DLILLC/Corbis, p.89cl Terry W. Eggers/Corbis, p.89bl Tom Brakefield/zefa/Corbis, p.89br Jeff Vanuga/Corbis, p.90-91 Tom Brakefield/Corbis, p.90bl Kevin Schafer/Corbis, p.91tr DLILLC/Corbis, p.91br Ronnie Kaufman/Corbis, p.92 Renee Lynn/Corbis, p.93t Martin Harvey/Corbis, p.93bl Konrad Wothe/Getty, p.93br Theo Allofs/Corbis, p.94-95 Gallo Images/Corbis, p.95tr Joseph Van Os/Getty, p.95c John Conrad/Corbis, p.95bl Gallo Images/Corbis, p.96-97 Gabriela Staebler/zefa/Corbis, p.96bl Ikachan /Dreamstime.com, p.97cr DLILLC/Corbis, p.97br Jazzer/Dreamstime.com, p.99b Joe McDonald/Corbis

Additional images used on sticker sheet: bottom row, first sticker: Dennis Sabo/Dreamstime.com

Index

A

Adapted 32
Allosaurus 60
Amazon 36-37
Amphibians 35
Anacondas 37
Angel sharks 7
Ankylosaurus 59
Anteaters 31, 34
Ants 34
Apatosaurus 60
Apes 31
Arms and Legs 58, 71
Attacks on humans 24
Australia 48-49

B

Babies 20, 21, 23, 64, 66, 84, 85
Balance 12
Bandicoots 49
Bats 31, 36
Beaks 61
Biggest Dinosaur 54
Biggest shark 9
Biggest wild cat 79
Birds 31, 32, 33, 37, 42, 44, 48
Blood 17, 24, 36
Blue sharks 14-15, 21
Bobcats 83
Bones 55, 60, 67
Brachiosaurus 61
Breathing 6
Buffalo 91
Bull shark 24

C

Camouflage 7, 34
Canopy 31
Capybaras 36
Cartilage 6
Cassowaries 48
Ceratosaurus 62
Cheetahs 79, 81
Chameleons 40
Chimpanzees 38
Claws 88
Clouded leopards 43
Clubs 59
Coats 78, 79, 81, 90, 95
Cobras 44, 46
Colors 80, 81
Congo 40-41
Conifers 56
Cookie-cutter sharks 11
Coral snakes 47
Cretaceous period 57
Crocodiles 31
Cubs 84-85, 89, 95

D

Death of the Dinosaurs 72-73
Deinonychus 69
Deer 91
Dens 95
Deserts 83
Diplodocus 57
Diving 19
Dogfish 7, 21

113

Index

E
Ears 17, 81, 89
Egg cases 20, 21
Eggs 20, 21, 64, 65
Electric signals 17
Eoraptor 56
Equator 31
Extinct 72
Eyes 8, 17, 23

F
Families 20-21, 64-65, 69, 84-87
Fastest shark 8
Fastest wild cat 79, 81
Fathers 86, 87
Feeding 9, 15, 18, 22, 33, 34, 36, 37, 44, 47, 91
Ferns 63
Fins 12, 25
Fish 6, 9, 11, 13, 14, 15, 17, 18, 31, 32, 33, 43
Forests 57, 82, 83, 95
Forest Floor 30, 31, 47
Fossils 55
Frills 66, 67
Frogs 31, 35, 47, 49
Fur 78, 83, 93, 97

G
Giganotosaurus 54
Gills 6
Golden lion tamarins 32
Gorillas 40
Grasslands 86, 95
Great white sharks 9, 11, 18-19, 24

H
Habitat destruction 96
Harpy eagles 33
Hammerhead sharks 8, 17, 22-23
Hearing 16, 88, 89
Herds 61, 63
Hunting 14, 16-17, 18, 19, 34-35, 68-69, 78, 85, 86, 88-89, 91, 95, 96
Hypselosaurus 65

I
Iberian lynxes 97
Iguanodon 68, 69
Indian gharials 33
Indonesia 44-45
Insects 31, 34, 37, 41

J
Jaguars 34, 82, 83
Jaws 6, 60, 70, 88
Jurassic period 57

K
Kangaroos 49
Killer whales 19
Killing sharks 25

L
Lateral lines 16
Lemon sharks 21
Leopards 81, 94-95
Lionesses 86
Lions 78, 85, 86-87

Lynxes 81, 97

M
Maiasaura 64, 65
Mako sharks 8
Mammals 32, 78
Mandrills 38
Manes 78, 87
Margays 42
Mate 14
Meat eaters 78
Meat-eating dinosaurs 55, 58, 60, 70
Megalodon 13
Megalosaurus 55
Mermaid's purses 21
Mesozoic era 57
Milk 85
Millipedes 41
Monkeys 31, 33, 38-39, 42
Mosses 56
Mothers 20, 21, 23, 64, 65, 84, 85, 87, 89, 95
Mountain lions (pumas) 81
Mountains 83, 95
Museums 55

N
Necks 61
Nests 65
Nurse sharks 10, 11

O
Ocean floor 7, 20
Ocelots 43, 80
Okapi 40
Orangutans 44
Ornithopod dinosaurs 61
Owl monkeys 39

P
Packs 69
Palm trees 56
Paw prints 93
Peacocks 44
Periods 56, 57
Piranha 33
Plant-eating dinosaurs 57, 59, 61, 63, 66, 68
Plants 56, 57, 63
Plateosaurus 59
Plates 59, 63
Play-fight 85
Poison dart frogs 35
Porbeagles 11
Predators 34
Prey 10, 11, 37, 46, 58, 71, 88, 89, 91, 94, 95
Prides 86, 87
Primates 38
Pups (babies) 18, 20-21, 23
Pygmy marmosets 39

R
Rain forests 30, 31, 36, 40, 44, 48
Reptiles 32, 33, 54
Reserves 96
Resting 86, 94, 95
Rhinoceros beetles 37
Roaring 86, 92
Rodents 36

S
Scent 42, 93
Scottish wild cats 79
Schools 22
Senses 16-17, 88
Servals 89

Index

Siberian tigers 79, 90
Sight 17, 88
Skeletons 6, 55
Skulls 67
Sloths 31, 33
Smell 17, 23, 88
Snakes 31, 37, 44, 46-47
Snow leopards 83, 97
Space rocks 72, 73
Species 80
Spikes 58, 62, 68
Spines 59
Spots 34, 80, 81, 85, 95
Spraying 93
Stars, exploding 72
Steering 12
Stegosaurus 62-63
Stingrays 22
Stripes 80, 90
Surfboards 25
Swimbladders 13
Swimming 8, 11, 12-13, 14, 15, 19, 23, 24, 90

T

Tails 7, 10, 11, 12, 13, 59, 62, 79, 81, 82
Teeth 10, 13, 19, 54, 55, 60, 67, 70
Termites 34
Territory 92, 93
Thresher sharks 11
Thumbs 68
Tigers 42, 79, 80, 89, 90-91
Tiger sharks 11, 24
Touch 16

Tourists 96
Tracking Wild Cats 93
Trapping and killing Wild Cats 90, 96, 97
Tree climbing 82, 91, 94
Tree frogs 49
Tree kangaroos 48
Tree snakes 47
Triassic period 56, 57
Triceratops 66-67
Turtles 31
Tyrannosaurus Rex 67, 70-71

V

Vampire bats 36
Velociraptor 57, 58
Volcanoes 73

W

Water dragons 45
Water holes 87
Whale sharks 9
Wobbegongs 7

Y

Yolk 21

Z

Zebras 86, 89